Bhajanamritam

2017 Supplement

Mata Amritanandamayi Center
San Ramon, California, USA

Bhajanamritam Supplement 2017

Published By:
Mata Amritanandamayi Center
P.O. Box 613, San Ramon, CA 94583-0613
USA
www.amma.org

First printing by MA Center: April 2017

Address in India:
Mata Amritanandamayi Mission Trust
Amritapuri, Kollam Dt.
Kerala 690546, India
www.amritapuri.org
inform@amritapuri.org

Europe: www.amma-europe.org

About Pronunciation

The following key is for the guidance of those who are unfamiliar with the transliteration codes used in this book:

A	-as	a	in America
AI	-as	ai	in aisle
AU	-as	ow	in how
E	-as	e	in they
I	-as	ea	in heat
O	-as	o	in or
U	-as	u	in suit
KH	-as	kh	in Eckhart
G	-as	g	in give
GH	-as	gh	in loghouse
PH	-as	ph	in shepherd
BH	-as	bh	in clubhouse
TH	-as	th	in lighthouse
DH	-as	dh	in redhead
CH	-as	ch-h	in staunch-heart
JH	-as	dge	in hedgehog
Ñ	-as	ny	in canyon
Ś	-as	sh	in shine
Ṣ	-as	c	in efficient
Ṅ	-as	ng	in sing, (nasal sound)
V	-as	v	in valley
ZH	-as	rh	in rhythm
R	-as	r	in ride

Vowels with a line on top are pronounced like the vowels listed above but held twice as long.

The letters with dots under them (ṭ, ṭh, ḍ, ḍh, ṇ) are palatal sounds. They are pronounced with the tip of the tongue against the hard palate.

Table of Contents

Ammā ammā enum (Tamil) 6
Ammā dēvi (Tulu version) 6
Amṛtalayam ānandalayam (Malayalam) 7
Antardarśanattinuḷḷa (Malayalam) 8
Anudinamum (Tamil) 9
Arikiluṇḍenkilum (Tamil version) 10
Bārayya śiva (Kannada) 11
Bhuvanasundarī (Tamil) 12
Cinna cinna kaṇṇā (Tamil) 13
Dānavāntakā rāmā (Kannada) 15
Engum annaiyun (Tamil) 16
Ennai nān maranda (Tamil) 16
En mannassiloru maunam (Tamil) 17
Gajānanā he gajānanā (Tamil) 18
Gōkula bālā gōvindā (Malayalam) 18
Gopiyara usirē (Kannada) 19
He śrīnivāsa (Kannada) 20
Indu nammamma (Kannada) 21
Iniyoru janmam (Kannada version) 22
Inkē irukkum (Tamil) 23
Kāḷi māteyē (Kannada) 24
Kaṇṇeḍuttu pārammā (Tamil) 25
Kaṇṇan kaḷḷa kaṇṇan (Tamil) 26
Kārunya rupiṇi (Malayalam) 27
Kalamurali (Tamil version) 28
Kāruṇya murtte (Kannada version) 28
Kaṭaikkaṇ pārvai (Tamil) 29

Kāvaṭiyām kāvaṭi (Tamil) 30
Kayilaiyilē śivaperumān (Tamil) 31
Kṣaṇakṣaṇavu (Kannada) 32
Kuzhandaiyena (Tamil) 33
Kṛṣṇa kanaiyyā (Malayalam) 34
Muttu mūkkutti (Tamil) 35
Nān enbatai (Tamil) 36
Nānendu kāṇuve (Kannaḍa) 37
Nanna hudōṭṭada (Kannada) 38
Nannōḍeya (Kannada) 39
Orunāḷum piriyātta (Kannada version) 39
Neñcakaṁ ventiṭunnu (Malayalam) 40
Pādāravindakē (Kannada) 41
Ponnammā en ammā (Tamil) 42
Sāmbasadāśiva (Tamil) 43
Parinamamiyallatta (Kannada version) 43
Śivke (Hindi) 44
Śri dēvi laḷitā (Tamil) 45
Taḷarnnuraṅgukayō (Malayalam) 47
Tañcam undan (Tamil) 48
Tāṇḍavamāṭi (Tamil) 49
Taye tava (Kannada version) 50
Ulagamāga māri nirkkum (Tamil) 51
Ulakattin tāyenṭru (Tamil) 52
Unai maravā varamonḍru (Tamil) 53
Uyara uyara (Tamil) 54
Uyirōṭuyirāy (Tamil) 55
Vaṭavṛkṣmām (Malayalam) 56

Ammā ammā enum (Tamil)

ammā ammā enum mandiram - adu
anaivarukkum sondamāna mandiram
summā adai colli colli pārunka
sorggam pōla vāzhvamaiyum kēḷunka

The mantra 'Mother' belongs to one and all. By the mere chanting of this mantra, life becomes a heaven.

aḷḷa aḷḷa kuraiyāda anbu tān
anaittuyirum sondamenum paṇbu tān
kaḷḷamellām pōkkukindhra kanivu tān
kāṇpavarkku makizhvu tarum kaḷippu tān

Her love never decreases. Her nature is to treat all beings as Her own. Her compassion is the destroyer of envy, and Her presence makes everyone joyful.

mella mella nammaiyavaḷ māttruvāḷ
mēnmai tarum pādayinau kāṭṭuvāḷ
solla solla inikkumavaḷ nāmam tān
solli pārttāl nāṭi varum kṣemam tān

Gradually She changes us and shows us the path of upliftment. Repeatedly chanting Her name brings sweetness and prosperity.

āṭuvōm... pāṭuvōm...
āṭi pāṭi anudinam koṇḍāṭuvōm
tudittāṭi pāṭi anudinam koṇḍāṭuvōm

Let's dance and sing, and make every day a celebration! Let's make every day a celebration glorifying Her!

Ammā dēvi (Tulu version)

ammā dēvi tānitantānā

dēvi dēvi tantana nīnā

irnā mukhada munkuruḷāṭṭā
miñcōntuppuna mandahāsa
irentūdu mātta madēttē - kāḷī... dēvī...

tattvaśāstra enku gottijji
sādhana sankalpa gottijji
iranmātra tūdu batteyān - durgē... dēvi...

iranā bālē yānammā
īratte ēnkḷēgu māttalā
taṭadāne yenan tūvarē - caṇḍī... dēvī...

Amṛtalayam ānandalayam (Malayalam)

amṛtalayam ānandalayam
en ātmāvu śruticērum madhuralayam
pūvum prakṛtiyum pōle
ponnalakaḷum kaṭalum pōle
śruti cērumī laya bhangiyil
śruti cērumī laya bhangiyil

My soul is content and immersed in bliss - like a flower within nature, like waves within the ocean. I am immersed in sweet song.

pramada mānasavaniyil viriyum saugandhikaṅgaḷil
nī viral toṭumbōḷ praṇavamantra
dhvanikaḷuṇarum oru tamburuvāy mārum
praṇava tamburuvāy mārum
divya tamburuvāy mārum

At the touch of Your fingers, the flowers growing in the garden of my mind transform into a tambura playing the Omkara.

ātma harṣam tuḷumbi nilkkum
indīvaradaḷa śobha pōlum
nin nayanaṅgaḷil manassinde cippiyil
muttukaḷ tīrkkum oru māya mantramuṇḍō?
divya māya mantramuṇḍō?
dēvī māya mantramuṇḍō?

When the glance from Your lotus eyes shining with bliss falls upon me does it not have the power to create a pearl within the shell of my heart?

Antardarśanattinuḷḷa (Malayalam)

antardarśanattinuḷḷa cintayum prayatnavum
varttamāna hṛttilum pravṛddhamānamākki nī
antarangatantriyil prapañcasāramantramāy
sañcariccituṇnu nī svatantrabhāvadhārayāy

Even in current times, You inspire people to strive for self-realization. You are the Omkara mantra in the soul of every man. As said by the scriptures, You are the absolute.

āgamiccezhiccuninnulaññazhiññupōvatin
āgamōktiyōrkkilō nidānabinduvāṇu nī
āgamam vidhiccatokke ācariccupōkilum
ākulaṁ śamikkuvān bhavāni, nin kṛpāśrayaṁ

Only if self-effort is blessed by the grace of the Guru will we attain realization. In the heart blossoming with innocent love, You are the essence of poetry

bhaktiyāluṇarnnularnna niṣkkaḷanka cētasil
śuddhabhāvavaikharī nisargakāvyadhāra nī
maṇṇilēkkurannolicca veṇṇilāvupōle yenn-
-uḷḷil nin madhusmitābha sāndrasaukumāryamāy

When the mind is moving, You act as the force of creation. In a still mind, You shine as the power of God.

cittatārcalikkavē kriyātmakatvaśaktī nī
niścalam vasikkavē śivatvamennariññiṭām
śaktiyum śivatvavum parasparānupūrakam
buddhiyekkaviñña, vēda tattvasāramē, tozhām

Creativity and stillness are mutually complementary. I bow down before You, who are above the intellect and embody the essence of the Vedas.

Anudinamum (Tamil)

anudinamum unai ninaindu urugudamma neñjam - adu
arukil nindru ezhil mukhattai kaṇḍu rasikka keñjum
tiruvaruḷai tēḍivandun tiruvaḍiyil tañjam - guru
vaḍivām tāy umayē unai aravaṇaittu koñjum

Thinking of You daily, my heart melts. I yearn to move close to You and enjoy Your beautiful face. Seeking divine grace, I reached and took refuge at Your feet. O Goddess Uma, who are of the form of the Guru and Mother, we take comfort in Your embrace.

piñju manam unnaruḷāl parugum anbu vellam
neñjuruki unnizhalil nilai marandu tuḷḷum
añjukindra tīvinaikaḷ allal yāvum akalum - anku
pañjupōla manamiḷaki paramānandam koḷḷum

By Your grace, the waters of love have softened my mind and melted my heart, making me jump joyfully in abandon. All the fears and miseries that affected me have disappeared. My tender heart has attained supreme bliss.

aruḷamudē! ānandamē!
anbin vaḍivē! aḍaikkalam nīyē!

O Mother of grace! O blissful One, embodiment of love! You are my refuge!

māyaiyadin piḍiyinilē matiyizhandu uzhalum
makkaḷ manam amaidipera nin kazhalinai nizhalum
sēykaḷ nilai uyara un tiruvizhi malarndaruḷum - anbu
tāyundan sannidhikku taraṇi ellām tiraḷum

Those ensnared by Maya (cosmic delusion) act without discernment. To find peace of mind, they seek solace at Your feet. Your divine gaze uplifts souls. Hence, millions flock to Your divine presence, O loving Mother.

unadu padam dinamum manam paṇindiḍa manankanivāy
ninadaruḷāl paramapada nilai aḍaindiḍa aruḷvāy
guruvaḍivē tiruvaruḷē parivuḍan emai kāppāy - nān
maraimuḍiyinil maruvum nindan padamalaraḍi sērppāy

O Mother, bless us so that we may worship Your feet daily. By Your grace, may we reach the abode of the Supreme. O Divinity in the form of the Guru, protect us with love and affection. Help us attain Your feet, which hides the precious gems of the four Vedas.

Arikiluṇḍenkilum (Tamil version)

arugilirundum arindiṭa iyalāmal
alaigintrēn ammā
kaṇgaḷirundum kāṇaviyalāmal
tēṭugintrēn ammā... unnai
tēṭugintrēn ammā

mārgazhi iravil nīlavānil pūtta
veṇmadi nītānō...
vānattai sēra muṭiyāmal karaiyil
talaimōdum alaiyāga nān – ammā
talaimōdum alaiyāga nān

ulagattin sukhamellām nilaikkādenṭruḷḷa
uṇmaiyai uṇarndadinālē...
iravum pagalum kaṇṇīr perugi
ariyattuṭittēn ammā - unnai
ariyattuṭittēn ammā

tuyarattin sumaiyāl tuvaṇḍiṭum enniṭam
ārudal aḷittiṭa vārāy
varuvāy enḍruḷḷa āsaiyuṭan nān
nittamum kāttirukkinḍrēn - ammā
nittamum kāttirukkinḍrēn

Bārayya śiva (Kannada)

bārayya śivā bārayya śivā bārayya śivanē
nōḍuvē ninna manadaṇiye bārayya śivanē

Please come, my dear Lord Shiva. Let me behold You to my heart's content.

kailāsadi vāsipane umākāntanē
rudrākṣiya dharisihanē nīlakaṇṭhanē
bhaktarige oliyuva paramēśvaranē
nōḍuvē ninna manadaṇiye bārayya śivanē

Consort of Uma, You reside in Kailash. O blue-throated One, You wear the rudrākṣa bead. O supreme Lord, You readily offer boons to devotees. Let me behold You to my heart's content.

ruṇḍamāla dharisihane rudrēśvaranē
gangēyannu hottiruva śaśiśēkharanē
bhaktarige oliyuva paramēśvaranē
nōḍuvē ninna manadaṇiye bārayya śivanē

O fearsome One, You are adorned with a garland of skulls. Your wear the crescent moon on Your head, from which flows the cascading Ganga River. O supreme Lord, You readily offer boons to devotees. Let me behold You to my heart's content.

triśūlava hiḍidiha trilōkanāthanē
śmaśānadi vāsipanē bhūtanāthanē
bhaktarigē oliyuva paramēśvaranē
nōḍuvē ninna manadaṇiye bārayya śivanē

Lord of the three worlds, You wield the trident. O Lord of ghouls, You dwell in charnel grounds. Supreme Lord, You readily offer boons to devotees. Let me behold You to my heart's content.

śaśidhara śikhinētrā purahara girivāsā
trinayana suranāthā jaya! hara! jitakāmā

Victory to Shiva, whose head is adorned with a crescent moon, who has the eye of fire, who destroyed the demon known as Pura, who dwells in the mountain, who is three-eyed, who is Lord of the gods, and who has conquered desire.

Bhuvanasundarī (Tamil)

bhuvanasundarī śankaran tuṇaivi
ṣaṇmukhan vaṇankiṭum umayē – ammayē
ṣaṇmukhan vaṇankiṭum umayē
sahaja samādhi nilayē

O Uma You are the beauty of the universe. You are the consort of Lord Shankara. You are worshipped by Lord Shanmukha, Your son. You are ever dwelling in a state of supreme bliss.

tāmarai kaṇkaḷ amaiti tarum – atu
karuṇaiyinālē nīr tatumbum
mānuṭa janmattin poruḷ vizhantāl nī
bōdhippatellām atil teḷiyum

Your lotus like eyes bestow peace of mind. They are filled with crystalline tears because of Your exceeding compassion. If one desires to understand the meaning of human life, all that You teach will be shining in Your eyes.

malayinai kuṭaintu vīṭamaippāḷ - anku
katavinai tirantu varavērpāḷ
tāyavaḷ namakkena kāttiruppāḷ - nam
varukaiyinālē akam kuḷirvāḷ

You abide in mountain caves, and keep the doors open so as to receive everyone. O Mother, You await our arrival at the door. You will feel exhilarated upon seeing us arrive.

kēśavan sōdarī gajamukhan ammai nī āpadbāndhavi
anātharakṣaki bhārggavi saundari ambikai īśvari
mugguṇa māyai nīkkiṭum tāy nī tavattiru tēnmozhi
muttamizh kalaiyē sattāna poruḷē ānanda bhairavi
ammē ānanda bhairavi

You are the sister of Keshava and Mother of Gajamukha. You are the protector at all times, the savior of the destitute! You are the Mother that destroys the illusion of the three gunas. You are the exponent of the three arts, and the power behind everything. O Mother, You are the Goddess of bliss!

Cinna cinna kaṇṇā (Tamil)

cinna cinna kaṇṇā sinkārakaṇṇā
cintaiyil kalandiṭum kārmēghavarṇṇā
cinnañciru itazhināle anpumozhi pēsavā
sīraṭṭi pāraṭṭi pālūṭṭi tālāṭṭa ōḍi vā kaṇṇā

O little Kanna (Krishna), beautiful Kaṇṇā, Your dark-hued form merges into the mind. Utter a few loving words with those tender lips! Come running, O Kaṇṇā, so that we may cuddle and praise You, give You some milk, and sing You a lullaby.

yaśōdayin karampiḍittu taḷirnaḍai naḍantāy
yārumariyā līlaiseydu makkaḷai kāttāy
yātumariyā siruppiḷḷayāy viḷaiyāḍinai
yādavā mādhavā māyavā kṛṣṇā
yādavā mādhavā māyavā manamōhana kṛṣṇā

You toddled, holding Yashoda's hand. Engaging in divine play without anyone's knowledge, You saved the people. You frolic like an innocent, little child. O Yadava, Madhava, who wields the power of illusion, You captivate the mind!

tunpam tarum asurarai māyaiyāl māittāy
kurumpāle gōpiyarai anpuḍan īrttāy
enna nī seydālum unnōḍu kōpamillaiyē
ennavā mannavā cinnavā kṛṣṇā
ennavā mannavā cinnavā śrī bālakṛṣṇā

With Your power of illusion, You destroyed the evil demons. And with Your loving mischief, You captivated the milkmaids' hearts. No matter what You do, we can never get angry with You, O Lord, little One, child Krishna!

piñjukālāl nañjutarum kāḷiyanai azhittāy
añjaneñcil tañjamtandu ānandam aḷittāy
inampuriyā makizhvaḷitta uravāṭināy
anpane naṇpane āyanē kṛṣṇā
anpane naṇpane āyanē gōvindakṛṣṇā

With those tender feet, You stamped out the ego of the poisonous Kaliya snake. You bestow bliss that removes fear from the heart and that grants refuge. You forge a bond that confers indescribable bliss, O Companion, Friend, cowherd Krishna!

Dānavāntakā rāmā (Kannada)

dānavāntakā rāmā
dāśarathē raghu rāmā
dīna dayaḷō rāmā
dhīra vīra śrī rāmā

O Rama, destroyer of demons, son of Daśaratha, and scion of the Raghu dynasty, You are compassionate to the fallen. You are wise and valorous.

rāmā jaya jaya rāmā, rāmā jānaki rāmā
rāmā paṭṭābhi rāmā, rāmā kōdaṇḍa rāmā

Victory to Rama, consort of Janaki! You hold arrows, and are heir to the throne.

prēmabhakti tā rāmā
prārabdhava kaḷe rāmā
pavana suta priyanē rāmā
parama pāvanā rāmā

O Rama, give me love and devotion, and remove my karmic burden. Beloved of Hanuman, You are of utmost purity.

vairāgya taḷeso rāmā
viśva caitanya rāmā
vārija nayanā rāmā
vāmadēva sakha rāmā

O Rama, who is the divine consciousness of the universe, give me dispassion. O lotus-eyed One, You are Lord Shiva's friend.

niṣkāmi māḍo rāmā
nisvārthi māḍo rāmā
nirupama guṇanē rāmā
nityānandane rāmā

O Rama, grant me freedom from desires and selflessness. O Lord of incomparable virtues, You are ever blissful.

Engum annaiyun (Tamil)

engum annaiyun vaṭivām
edilum annaiyun vaṭivām
ponkum kaṭalilum pudunilavadilum
pozhundiṭum un ezhil amudām...

Mother, Your form pervades everywhere. Your form pervades everything. The rising ocean and moon light shower Your nectarean beauty.

makkaḷin manam tanil oḷirvāy – nī
makizhvuṭan vāzhndiṭa aruḷvāy
kāttrāy mazhaiyāy kanalāy nilamāy
vānamumāy nī tikazhvāy

You shine in the hearts of Your children and bless them with a happy life. You manifest as breeze, rain, fire, earth and sky.

pārpukazh annai pādam tudittē
pāriṭamellām pāṭiṭuvōmē

Let us sing everywhere the glory of Your lotus feet!

Ennai nān maranda (Tamil)

ennai nān maranda vēḷai
unnaiyē ninaikka vēṇḍum
unnai nān maranda pōdum
ennil nī irukka vēṇḍum

When I forget myself, I should be thinking of You. Even if I forget You, You should remain with me.

kaṇṇil nī maṇiyumāvāy
karuttinil oḷiyumāvāy
uṇṇum poruḷ nīyumāvāy
ulakattin tāyumāvāy

enkenku senḍrālum en vizhi kāṇbadu
ammānin ponrūpamē

You are the pupil of my eye. You are the light of my thoughts. You are my nourishment, You are the Mother of the universe. O Mother, wherever I cast my eyes I see Your effulgent form

tāyāvāy makaḷumāvāy
tānkiṭum tōzhiyāvāy
anbirkku viḷakkamāvāy
ammā nī anaittumāvāy
enkenku senḍrālum en vizhi kāṇbadu
ammānin ponrūpamē

You are Mother, daughter and supportive friend, O embodiment of love, You are everything. O Mother, wherever I cast my eyes I see Your effulgent form.

En mannassiloru maunam (Tamil)

en manadil oru maunaṁ
maṇivaṇṇan varādadin maunaṁ
kaṇṇane kāṇādurugi urugiyen
kaṇgaḷil kaṇṇīr perugum

ānirai mēyttu varādadō - kaṇṇan
āzhtuyil nīnki ezhādadō
kārmukil vaṇṇanai kāṇattuṭikkumen
vāṭiya kōlam marandadō

pālveṇṇayum kiṭaikkādadō - piñcu
pādaṁ iṭari vizhundadō
nin malaraṭigaḷil tēn nukara
bhaktavaṇḍukaḷ mūṭi maraittadō

ēn vara tāmadaṁ innuṁ - kaṇṇan
ennai marandiruppānō
kaṇṇā varuganī kārmukilvaṇṇā - en
kaṇṇīr vizhigaḷin munnē

Gajānanā he gajānanā (Tamil)

gajānanā he gajānanā
gajānanā he gajavadanā

O Gajanana, elephant-faced Lord!

vezha mukhattu vināyakanē
viḷanku sindūra vināyakanē
aindu karankaḷ uṭayavanē
ankuśa pāśam koṇḍavanē

O elephant-faced Lord, destroyer of our miseries! You wear kumkum, have five arms and bear the goad and the noose.

aimpula vēṭkai aṭakkiṭuvāy
añcēl eṇṭrē kāttiṭuvāy
allalakaḷ nīkki aruḷ taruvāy
anbāl emmai āṇṭiṭuvāy

You keep our five senses in control. You show the mudra of fearlessness. You remove our worries and rule over us lovingly.

Gōkula bālā gōvindā (Malayalam)

gōkula bālā gōvindā
gōkula pālā gōvindā
gōpakumāra gōvindā
gōvindā hari gōvindā

O boy of Gōkul (cowherd clan), Protector of cows and the cowherd clan, cowherd boy, O Vishnu!

vārmuṭiyil cārttiyatārī
varṇṇappīli mayilppīli
vākaccārttinu vannavarō
vṛndāvanattile gōpikaḷō

Who adorned Your beautiful locks with the colorful, peacock feather? Was it those who came for the morning worship or the milkmaids of Vṛndāvan?

pūntānam nalkiyatallē
ponnuṇṇikkīvanamāla
mēlppattūr nalkiyatallē
muktakamāla maṇimāla

Wasn't it Puntanam who offered You, O darling Kṛṣṇa, the garland of wild flowers? Wasn't it Melppattur who offered You a poem of free verse?

tirumadhuram nēdikkām
tuḷasippūkkaḷ cūṭikkām
tarumō tarumō kārvarṇṇā
tāmarakkaiyyile tūveṇṇa

We shall offer You sweet pudding and tulasi (basil) flowers. O dark-hued One, won't You offer us some of the butter from Your lovely hands?

Gopiyara usirē (Kannada)

gopiyara usirē kṛṣṇa gōpālakṛṣṇa
govarddhanadhara kṛṣṇa gītānāyaka kṛṣṇa

The very life breath of the gopis, O Krishna, Gopala Krishna. The One who lifted the Govardhana Mountain, Lord of the Gita...

yaśoda nandana kṛṣṇa yadukulatilakane kṛṣṇa
yamunā taṭadī kṛṣṇa rāsavihāri kṛṣṇa

Son of Yashoda, King of the Yadukulas, the One at the banks of the Yamuna. The One who revels in the Rasa (the divine dance).

kṛṣṇā harē kṛṣṇā kṛṣṇā giridhara kṛṣṇā

O Krishna, O Hari...

sarōjanētrane kṛṣṇa ninnaya samayār kṛṣṇa
varṇisalasadaḷa kṛṣṇa guṇasāgaranē kṛṣṇa

Lotus-eyed Krishna, who can be equated with You? Krishna is beyond description, Krishna is the Ocean of divine qualities.

kṛpārdra hṛdayane kṛṣṇa karuṇārasanē kṛṣṇa
dāsara prāṇanē kṛṣṇa dāsara dāsanē kṛṣṇa

Your heart is soaked in grace, You are compassion personified. You are the soul of Your servants, and You are also the servant of Your servants.

He śrīnivāsa (Kannada)

he śrīnivāsa he ṛṣikēśa
karuṇadi pālisō hē pāṇḍuranga
bhavasāgaradi bendu bendu nondenayya
tande bandu salahayya śrī mukunda

O Srinivasa, O Rishikesa (names of Vishnu), please take care of us with compassion, O Panduranga. I've been in pain, burning in the ocean of transmigration. Please come and console me, O Sri Mukunda!

kāmakāñcanagaḷige mōhitanāgi nā
ninnanu stutisadē matihinanāde
janmada lakṣyava tiḷiyade vyartthavāgi
pāramārtthava toredu ninnane marete

I have been disillusioned by desire and greed. I was foolish for not remembering You. Not knowing the goal of this life, I wasted it. I forgot You and lost sight of the ultimate goal

hē śrīnivāsa hē ṛṣikēśa hē padmanābha hē pāṇḍuranga

O Srinivasa, O Rishikesa, O Padmanabha, O Panduranga!

mōhada baleyalli siluki oddāḍide
dāriya kāṇade baḷalide toḷalide
nijavanu aritu śaraṇu bandihenīga
tvaritadi kāyō hē pāṇḍuranga

I lost my way getting caught in the net of desires. I lost sight of my path and suffered for it. Now I understand the truth and I have come in surrender to You. Please come and save me right away!

viṭhala pāṇḍuranga viṭhala pāṇḍuranga

O Vithala, Panduranga! (names of Lord Vishnu)

Indu nammamma (Kannada)

indu nammamma na mūrige bandaḷu
harṣada varṣava karedihaḷu

Today my Mother has come to our town. She has brought down a rain of joy.

makkaḷa kāṇalu tavakisī nannamma
bēgane lōkava suttāṭi bandaḷu
hōdalli bantalli muddina maḷegaredu
duḥkhavu mithyavu entutā nuṭivaḷu

My Mother, eager to meet her children, travels all over the world at good speed. Wherever she goes she showers love and kisses, and tells us that sorrow is unreal.

kaicācci baḷigenna seḷedukoṇḍihaḷu
maṭilalī malagisī maidaṭa vidaḷu
muddū maguvē bhayapaṭadirentu
tabbimuddāṭī prasāda koṭṭaḷu

She stretched out her hand and pulled me to Her. She put me in Her lap and patted my back. She told me, darling child, don't be afraid. She hugged me, kissed me and gave me prasad

ībhavasāgara dāṭisu tāyē
dīnaḷa īmore kēḷamma tāye
mōhakke bedaruve kapaṭakke hedaruve
dāriya kāṇadē dikkeṭṭu aledihe

O Mother, help me cross this ocean of worldliness. O Mother, please listen to this helpless one. I fear attachment and I fear deceit. I have lost my way and am wandering aimlessly.

mithyava nīgū satyava tōrū
kattale nīgū beḷakannu tōru
mṛtyuva nīgū amṛtatva nīḍū
lōkakke śānti nīḍu – tāyē
samastake sukhava nīḍu tāyē

Lead us from untruth to truth; From darkness to light; From death to immortality. May all beings in all the worlds be happy.

Iniyoru janmam (Kannada version)

innondu janma nīḍadiru kṛṣṇa
madamōha rāṭige dūḍadiru
nīḍidare nina dāsānudāsiya
janmava enage karuṇisayyā

nina nāma manadali sthiravāgali kṛṣṇa
nina pādapatmā sadā beḷagali
sakalava ninna pratibheyāgi kanḍu
samaniladali mana sadā nillali
kṛṣṇa karuṇānidhē
karajōḍisi kaimugive

avaniyilupakāra pradavāgali janma
avināśa sukhadāna ennindāgali
adakāgi janma nīḍuve yādare
agaṇita narajanma enage nīḍu

Inkē irukkum (Tamil)

inkē irukkum unnaikkāṇā alaikirārē śankarā
enkēcentṛu etanai kāṇpār yārarivār śankarā
ankē inkē alaintu ōṭi taḷarumvarai śankarā
śankēseviṭan kātilpōla muzhankiṭumē śankarā

O Shankara, You are right here but people are wandering to see You elsewhere. Where will they go and what will they see? No one knows. People wander here and there till they get exhausted, like a conch sounding before deaf ears.

āśaiyatan āttralālē tavaruseyvār śankarā
arivin āttral kūṭumbōtu uṇarntiṭuvār śankarā
uṇarntavarō varuntumbōtu tiruntiṭuvār śankarā
tiruntiyavar unataruḷāl uyarntiṭuvār śankarā

O Shankara, people make mistakes because of the power of their desires. They realize this when their knowledge increases. They change themselves when they repent for their mistakes. Those changed people will reach a high status by Your grace.

tannil unnai kaṇḍukoḷḷa tavariyavar śankarā
mattravarai tāzhntavarāy kaṇḍiṭuvār śankarā
tannil unnai kaṇḍukoṇḍa uttamarō śankarā
enkum etilum unnaikkaṇḍu vaṇankiṭuvār śankarā

O Shankara, those who fail to see You in themselves will see others as inferior. Those great people who have seen You within worship You in each and every thing.

śankarā śiva śankarā śiva satguru nāthanē śankarā
śankarā śiva śankarā tiru kailāsa nāthanē śankarā

O Shankara, absolute One, Self-realized Master, Lord of Mount Kailash.

Kāḷi māteyē (Kannada)

kāḷi māteyē kāruṇya kīrtiyē
vāñchita phala dāteyē amṛtānanda mūrtiyē

O Mother Kali, You are renowned for Your compassion. Bestower of desires, You are of the form of immortality.

ninna makkaḷu nāvu namma irisu satya mārgadi
kaṣṭaveṣṭe barali koḍu śakti śānti nemmadi
svārtha biḍisi tyāga beḷesi naḍēsu namma avirata
kāma-krōdha mōha-lōbha mada-matsara kaḍiyuta

We are Your children. Please keep us on the true path. Let there be any amount of difficulties in our lives. Please give us strength and peace. Please remove selfishness and may the attitude of sacrifice grow in us. Keep us on this path incessantly. Please remove lust, anger, delusion, greed, pride and envy.

kali mā jai jai kāli mā
kāli mā jai jai durge mā

Victory to Mother Kali. Victory to Mother Durga.

janani ninna bēḍutihevu bhaktiyinda bhajipevu
irisu namma mukti-pathadi eḍebiḍadē satatavu
māyayinda dūramāḍu svārthavillade duḍivevu
sulabhamukti mārga tōru dēvi ninna stutipevu

O Mother, with devotional hymns, we beg You to always keep us on the path of salvation. Please keep delusion away from us, and we will strive selflessly. Kindly show the easy path to liberation while we sing Your glories.

Kaṇṇeḍuttu pārammā (Tamil)

kaṇṇeḍuttu pārammā, piḷḷai idu unadammā
sevi koḍuttu kēḷammā, tāy nī enadammā
bandhuvenḍru sondamenḍru vērevarum vēṇḍāmammā
tuṇaiyāka tāyē nīyē ennuḍen iruppāyammā

O Mother, look at me. I am Your child. Please listen to me. I am Your very own. I don't want any other kith or kin. O Mother, it will be enough if You remain with me.

pārvatiyē paripūraṇiyē śankariyē sarvēśvariyē

O Mother Parvati, Shankari, Goddess of all!

arivillai aramum illai pūjai tavam eduvum illai
sukhabhōga sindanaiyil un ninaivēdum vandadumillai
nal vākku sollittandu nal vazhi kāṭṭittandu
kai koḍuttammā nī enḍrumē kāttiḍuvāy

I have neither the wealth of wisdom nor good deeds. Mired in pleasure, I don't think of You. With kind words, please guide me, holding my hand, and protect me for all times.

pārvatiyē paripūraṇiyē śankariyē sarvēśvariyē

O Mother Parvati, Shankari, Goddess of all!

ennaiyē tandēn ammā unnaiyē taruvāy ammā
nān unnai aṭaiyum nāḷum eppōdu varumammā?
uyir veḍiyum vēḷai tāyē un darisanamē taruka
piravillā nilai tandu karai sēra varum taruka

I offer myself to You. Please give Yourself to me. When will we become one? In my last living moment, please grant me Your vision. Bless me with the boon of spiritual liberation so that I am never reborn.

pārvatiyē paripūraṇiyē śankariyē sarvēśvariyē

O Mother Parvati, Shankari, Goddess of all!

Kaṇṇan kaḷḷa kaṇṇan (Tamil)

yaśodayin cinna kaṇṇan
gōpiyarin cella kaṇṇan
bṛndāvanattin cuṭṭi kaṇṇan
enkaḷ uḷḷam kavarnta kaḷḷakaṇṇan

Little Krishna of Mother Yashoda, darling Krishna of the gopis! The mischievous Krishna of Vrindavan- the Krishna who has stolen our hearts!

kaṇṇan kaḷḷa kaṇṇan avanai
kaiyyum kaḷavumāy piṭittiṭa vēṇumaṭī kaḷḷa kaṇṇan
mella mella vantē uḷḷattai
sollāmalē koḷḷai koḷkindravan

Krishna, naughty Krishna! We should catch him red-handed... He will come slowly and steal our hearts without a warning.

ennē azhaku enpān – vekkattil
kaṇkaḷai mūṭum oru kaṇattinilē
kannam kiḷḷi celvān
peṇṇē un vīṭṭukkuḷḷē uriyil vaittirukkum
veṇṇaippānaiyinai tiṇṇam tiruṭi celvān

Lord Krishna will praise Your beauty and when you blush and close your eyes, He will pinch your cheeks and run away! O Gopi, He will surely steal all the butter pots from your house and run away!

rādhe rādhe kṛṣṇa kṛṣṇa rādhe govinda bhajo
rādhe gopāla bhajo rādhe kṛṣṇa

O Radha Krishna, Krishna! Sing the divine names of Radha and Govinda!

enna piḷḷai peṭrāy yaśoda
maṇṇum viṇṇum munnar kāṇāta
aṭṭahāsam tānkavillai

kaṭṭikarambu avan cuṭṭittanankaḷellām
muṭrum sahikkavillai tiṭṭa manam varavum illai
rādhe rādhe rādhe rādhe kṛṣṇa

O Yashoda, what a naughty son you have- His mischief is intolerable, unparalleled in the entire universe! Even though the sweet little One's mischief is hard to endure, the heart refuses to rebuke him!

Kārunya rupiṇi (Malayalam)

kārunya rupiṇi ammē
kāḷukayāṇende cittam
ninneyōrttalppavum kēzhān
prēmattin nīruravilla

O Mother, embodiment of compassion! My heart is craving to cry out in longing for You, but there are no flowing streams of love within me.

ērunnu mōhamitennum
śuddhasnēhamē ninne ariyān
māya tan mūṭupaṭam nī mātti
ennil teḷiyunnatennō?

The desire to know the pure love that is You is growing inside. When will You remove the veil of illusion and shine clearly within me?

śuddhasaundaryamē ninne kaṇḍu
uḷḷam kuḷirkkunnatennō?
ā maṭittaṭṭilī kuññu
viśramam koḷḷunnatennō?

O pure and beautiful form, when will my heart rejuvenate at Your sight? When will You allow this child of Yours to take rest in Your lap?

Kalamurali (Tamil version)

kuzhalisaiyāl emai mayakkum mukundā
nīyāṭum arankāgaṭṭum en manaṁ

pulavar punaindadu puṣpavimānaṁ
en uḷḷamē undan ratnavimānaṁ
īṭiṇaiyillā ezhilmigu vaiyam
nī naṭaṁ puriyum nāṭṭiya mēṭai

oru piṭi avalāl peruṁ pēraḷittāy
oru sir ilaiyai amudena koṇḍāy
tuyaraṁ migundu kaṇṇīr sindum
draupadikaḷ - tuyar nīkki aruḷvāy

eḷiyavarkkeṇtrum naṇbananṭrō nī
eḷiya kuzhalilum pozhivāy amudai
mayirpīli aṇiyum yadukula bālā
līlai seydālum yōgiyanṭrō nī

Kāruṇya murtte (Kannada version)

kāruṇya mūrtti śyāmala varṇṇā
kaṇṇu tereyō kṛṣṇā
duḥkhanivāraka nallave nī - ena
tāpava kaḷē kṛṣṇā

namagellā āśraya nīne
candāvare nayana śrīkṛṣṇa
pūjege anudina kambani haniyē
puṣpāñjalī ō kṛṣṇā
tāpava kaḷē kṛṣṇā

iruḷali baḷalide nānu
mānasamōhana gōpāla
īrēḷu lōkava āḷuva śrīdhara
kaṇṇu tereyō kṛṣṇā
tāpava kaḷē kṛṣṇā

Kaṭaikkaṇ pārvai (Tamil)

kaṭaikkaṇ pārvai ondrē pōtum
ammā untan aruḷ vizhiyāl
kanimozhi ondrē pōtumammā
kavailakaḷ parantōṭum
kavailakaḷ parantōṭum

A glance from the corner of Your divine eyes is enough, Your sweet words are enough, for our sorrows to vanish.

amma untan aruḷ pārvai
pala mozhi pēsiṭum, un seyalkaḷ ellāmammā
pala poruḷ uṇarttiṭum
pala poruḷ uṇarttiṭum

Mother Your divine glance speaks a lot of words. Mother all Your actions make us understand many truths.

sparišanam ondrē pōtumammā
akamatai kuḷirvittiṭum tiruvaṭi toṭṭa pozhutil
karma vinai parantōṭum
karma vinai parantōṭum

Mother Your touch is enough to cool and pacify our heart. Prostrating at Your divine feet rids us of the burden of our past deeds.

jai jagadīśvari jai bhuvanēśvari
jai paramēśvari jai amṛteśvari

Glory to the Goddess of the universe, glory to the supreme Goddess, glory to the eternal Goddess!

Kāvaṭiyām kāvaṭi (Tamil)

kāvaṭiyām kāvaṭi kantavēlan kāvaṭi
śēvarkoṭi azhakanukku vaṇṇamayil kāvaṭi
vēdanaiyē vāzhkaiyalla bhaktiyatu urutuṇaiyē
vēṇḍutalāy vēlavan sannidhiyil kāvaṭi

Come let us offer kavadi (ceremonial offering) to Lord Murugan. Let us offer the multi-hued peacock kavadi to the beautiful Lord whose flag bears the symbol of a rooster. Life need not be full of sorrows, devotion to the Lord ensures protection. Let us offer kavadi in the divine presence of One who holds the spear.

pālum tēnum pañcāmṛta kāvaṭi
pazhamum śarkkarayum vibhūtiyil kāvaṭi
candana kāvaṭiyum puṣpakāvaṭiyum
ṣaṇmukhan sannidhiyil azhaku kāvaṭi

Let us offer kavadi of milk, honey, and panchamritam. Let us offer kavadi of fruits, jaggery and sacred ash. Let us offer kavadi of sandalwood, kavadi of flowers. Let us offer beautiful kavadi in the divine presence of Lord with six faces!

kāvaṭiyāṭu kandan cēvaṭi tēṭu
kāvaṭiyāṭu kumaran tiruvaṭi nāṭu
karuṇai vēlan ārmukhan malaraṭi tēṭu

Kavadi seeks the holy feet of Lord Kandan (vanquisher of mighty foes). Kavadi seeks the divine feet of Kumaran (eternal youth), the lotus feet of the compassionate Lord Velan with six faces.

tinayum tiraviya pannīrāl kāvaṭi
maccamūm sarppamum iḷanīrāl kāvaṭi
mayūra kāvaṭiyum santāna kāvaṭiyum
śaravaṇan sannidhiyil muttu kāvaṭi

Let us offer kavadi of millets, money and rose water, kavadi of fish, snake and coconut water. Let us offer peacock kavadi and sandalwood kavadi. Let us offer pearl kavadi in the auspicious presence of Lord Muruga!

iṭumbanavan eṭuttānē mutal kāvaṭi
irupuramāy tōḷinilē sumantānē kāvaṭi
śivagiri orupuramum śaktigiri marupuramum
śivaśakti pālanin vēlkāvaṭi

Like the demon devotee Idumba who carried the pearl kavadi, I carry the kavadi on either side of my shoulders. One side represent Shivagiri and the other Shakti giri. Vel (spear) kavadi of the son of Shiva and Shakti!

Kayilaiyilē śivaperumān (Tamil)

kayilaiyilē śivaperumān
uṭanuraiyum umaiyavaḷē
tuyilizhantu entan uḷḷam, vāṭuvatai ariyāyō?

O Goddess Uma living with Lord Shiva in Kailash, don't You know that our hearts are becoming parched, foregoing sleep?

mañcaḷilē piṭittuvaitta
piḷḷaiyinau koñcukirāy
añcavaikkum kōpakkāra
kumaranaiyum keñcukirāy
intapiḷḷai iḷayapiḷḷai
eṭuppārtaṁ kaippiḷḷai
nontapōtu vantaṇaikka
tāymanatil īramillai

You pamper Ganesha (whose form is moulded using turmeric) and beg fearsome and strong tempered Subrahmanya (not to leave Mount Kailash). Yet when this youngest child is suffering, Mother's heart dries up, She doesn't come to hug me...

ennainalla piḷḷaiyākka
annaiyāṭum nāṭakamō
erimalaipōl kōlamkāṭṭi
irankuvatum unmanamō
enakkāka vēṇḍavillai
nānarivēn tāymanatai
piṇakkāka nīṭippatu
unperumaikkazhakumillai

Mother is playing this drama to make me a good child. After showing Your form as lava Your heart comes down. I am not praying for myself. I know Mother's heart. It is not good for Your reputation if this dispute continues.

Kṣaṇakṣaṇavu (Kannada)

kṣaṇakṣaṇavu anukṣaṇavu
makkaḷa smaraṇe māḍuva
makkaḷigāgi bāḷuva dēviya
kaṇḍīdirā... kēḷīdirā – ō nōḍīdirā

Do you know of a Goddess who is always thinking of her children and is living a life for the sake of her children? Have you heard of such a One, have you seen such a One?

mantrarūpiṇi ātmarūpiṇi
caitanyarūpiṇi dēviya
ānandarūpiṇi śaktiya ammana
kaṇḍīdirā... kēḷīdirā – ō nōḍīdirā

She is the form of mantra, the embodiment of the Self. She is in the form of consciousness, She is Mother. Have you heard of such a One, have you seen such a One?

śvāsaniśvāsavu nisvārtthadegāgi
mī... saliṭṭiha dēviya
ellarigāgi bāḷuva tāyiya

kaṇḍīdirā... kēḷīdirā – ō nōḍīdirā

Have you come across such a Goddess who has devoted Her every breath for selflessness, and is living for the sake of everybody? Have you heard of such a One, have you seen such a One?

Kuzhandaiyena (Tamil)

kuzhandaiyena umayē unai pārāṭṭavā
āruyirē mārbil unai tālāṭṭavā
bālāmbikai dēvi tripurasundari
bālādēvi śrī śōḍaśi

O Bala Devi, Sri Shodashi, soul of my soul, shall I worship You as the 'little Goddess'? Shall I sing You a lullaby, holding You close to me?

makaranta maṇamsērttu pūñcōlai koṇarntu
muttē nān pūcchūṭṭi koṇḍāṭavā
kapaṭamillāmal nī kulunki sirittāy
kaṇpaṭṭiṭum kannattil poṭṭu vaikkavā
kaṇpaṭṭiṭum kannattil poṭṭu vaikkavā

Along with the perfumed jasmine, shall I fetch colorful flowers to decorate Your tresses?! Seeing Your innocent laughter, the evil eye may fall upon You- shall I keep You safe from harm by putting a black kohl dot on Your chin? (Indian tradition)

ponnāna pādaṅkaḷ puṇṇākiṭāmal
en kaikaḷ nilam vaittu vazhi amaikkavā
koñcum calankaikaḷ isaiyil nī mayanki
ōṭātē kaṇṇē urankiṭavā
ōṭātē kaṇṇē urankiṭavā

Walking on the bare ground Your golden feet may get hurt; shall I lay a path with my palms for You to walk on? Wanting to hear the jingling of Your anklets, You are running hither and thither; please come back and rest!

Kṛṣṇa kanaiyyā (Malayalam)

nāhaṁ vasāmi vaikuṇṭhe
yogināṁ hṛdaye na ca
mad bhaktā yatra gāyanti
tatra tiṣṭhāmi nārada, tatra tiṣṭhāmi nārada

'I dwell neither in Vaikuntha nor in the hearts of the yogins, but I dwell where my devotees sing my name, O Narada.'

kṛṣṇa kanaiyyā sundarabālā
vṛndāvana candrā vā, nīlamegha varṇṇā vā
nandakiśorā karmukil varṇṇā
rādhikalolā vā, rādhikālolā vā

O Krishna, beautiful boy, moon of Vrindavan, with the complexion of a blue cloud, come! Son of Nanda, dark-hued like a rain-cloud, Radha's delight, come!

bhaktacitta corā yaśodabālā
navanītacorā vā, kṛṣṇa navanītacorā vā
gopakumārā kāḷiyadamanā
sundara rūpā vā, sūndara rūpā vā

Stealer of the hearts of the devotees, child of Yashoda, butter thief, Krishna, come! Young cowherd boy, subduer of the serpent Kaliya, one with a beautiful form, come!

vaṁśīdhārī dvārakanāthā
muraḷīmanoharā vā, kṛṣṇa muraḷīmanoharā vā
sajjana sevita madanagopālā
govarddhana giridhārī govarddhana giridhārī

Bearer of the flute, Lord of Dvaraka, most enchanting flute player, come! You are served by good people, O delightful cowherd boy, and you lifted the Govardhana Mountain!

Muttu mūkkutti (Tamil)

muttu mūkkutti mukhattil minna nī muttam koṭukkaiyilē
anpu muttam manam kavarum ennai nī aṇaikkaiyilē
kavalaiyāl kalankum nān tiruppādam tozhutiṭavē
apalai nān enai marantē kaṇṇīrāl nanaittiṭuvēn

As You embrace me and bestow Your loving kiss, Your pearl nose-ring shines, and my mind is engulfed! Gripped with sorrow I bow down at Your divine feet; helpless I forget myself and drown in my tears.

muttamiṭṭu ivvulakai pūnkāvanamākkukirāy
anpu tantu tuyarakatti ezhilpūmiyākkukirāy
nīrōṭum nadiyinaiyum tīrtthamāka māttukindrāy
nī varaṇḍa idayattai gangayāka māttukindrāy

With Your love You transform the world into a garden. With Your love You remove all sorrow and make this world beautiful. You transform the flowing waters of the river into holy water. You transform the dry mind into the Ganges River.

vinaippayan kaṭantu mukti padam kāṭṭiṭavē
viyanulakil anpāna tāyena vantāyē
toṭuvatanām anaivarukkum marupiravi tantuviṭṭāy
piravāta perunilaiyai tāyē nī aruḷvāyē

Show me the path of liberation, help me transcend the cycle of karma, You who have come to this earth embodying motherly love. Your touch has transformed so many, made so many feel reborn. Please bestow Your boon that I may go beyond birth and death

vallavēḷa palluyirum enatāka vēṇḍum ammā
nallatāka kāṇpatellom nalamāka vēṇḍum ammā
uḷḷoḷiyē pēroḷiyāy ulakenkum katiroḷiyāy
narpirappām ippirappil nān kāṇa vēṇḍum ammā

I should be able to see myself in others, I should be able to see the good in everything. Help me realize, in this life, that the light glowing within me permeates the whole universe.

ammā unakku palakōṭi vandanankaḷ

Mother, I prostrate at Your holy feet over and over again.

Nān enbatai (Tamil)

nān enbatai marandāl – tān
yārenbatai uṇarntāl
nanmaikaḷ pirakkum namvazhi sirakkum
vanmaikaḷ oḍunkum akavazhi tirakkum

When we forget the false 'I' and realize the true 'I,' good qualities will dawn, our destiny will become better, sorrows will end, and the inner eye of wisdom will open.

uḍal enḍrum idu nilaiyillai
āḍal atil muzhu niraivillai
āḍal muḍintu tanai venḍrāl ānandamayamākumē

The body is ephemeral. One cannot derive total satisfaction from pleasures. If we can curb the vacillating mind and control the ego, we will enjoy bliss.

tēḍal enbatu mana ēkkam
vāḍal enbatu guṇamayakkam
tēḍal muḍintu tanaiyarindāl tūya manam malarumē

It is the mind's nature to seek. Sorrows are illusory. If we attain God after seeking, the pure mind will blossom.

pāḍal enbatu akamakizhvu
nāḍal enbatu iraiyuṇarvu
pāḍalilmūzhka meyyidanuḷ paraviḍum amaidiyē

Devotional hymns are an expression of inner happiness. Seeking is a sign of awakening God-consciousness. If we can immerse ourselves in devotional singing, peace will pervade the body.

ānandam pērānandam ānandam paramānandam
ānandam nityānandam ānandam ātmānandam

Bliss, immense bliss, supreme bliss, eternal bliss, bliss of the Self!

Nānendu kāṇuve (Kannaḍa)

nānendu kāṇuve ninna divya rūpava kṛṣṇā
ninagāgi kādiruve bahaḷa dinagaḷinda
nānu gaidaparādhavēnu ninninda dūraviralu
ī agalike tāḷalāre bēga bā nannoḍeyā

When shall I see Your divine form, O Krishna? I have been waiting for so long! What did I do wrong to make You stay away from me? I cannot bear this estrangement. Please come quickly to me!

tōride ninna puṭṭa bāyoḷu viśvavanne yaśōdege
viśvarūpava tōride arjunage raṇarangadi
pāda sēvakanige nīḍu ninna bhavya darśana
karuṇe tōru kṛṣṇā ī caraṇa dāsana mēlē

You opened Your lovely mouth to reveal the whole universe to Mother Yashoda. You revealed Your universal form to Arjuna on the battlefield. Please grant Your servant Your darśan. I have been serving Your feet.

yādava nātha gōkula nāthā jagannāthā kṛṣṇā

O Krishna, You are chief of the Yadava clan, leader of the cowherd clan, and Lord of the universe.

dhruva prahlādage nīḍide nī divya jñānavā
paramamitra kucēlana dāridryava kaḷēdē
nanagāvudu bēḍa ninna darśana bhāgyava biṭṭu
taḍavinnēkē prabhuve kṛpeyā mādi uddharisu

You bestowed divine knowledge on Dhruva and Prahlada. You

banished the poverty of Your dear friend Kuchela. I want nothing but Your darshan. Without further delay, please shower Your grace and liberate me.

Nanna hudōṭṭada (Kannada)

nanna hudōṭṭada mallige sampigē
ammani gāgiyē nagutālivē
nanna mane bīdiya podegaḷā hūgaḷu
ammanī gāgiyē araḷidāvē

The jasmines and champaks in my garden are smiling for Mother's sake. The flowers in bushes on my street have bloomed for Mother's sake.

nannayī ūrina maragiḍa baḷḷiyu
ammani gāgiyē kādidāvē
nannayī nāḍina hasirēle hūhaṇṇu
ammanī gāgiye biriyutīvē

The trees and vines and plants of my town are waiting for Mother's sake. The green leaves, fruits and flowers of my land have been borne for Mother's sake.

nannayī bhūmiya ondondu jīviyu
ammani gāgiye jīvisive
nannayī lōkada acarācara vella
ammani gāgiyē tapisutīvē

Each and every being of this Earth of mine are living on for Mother's sake. Every one of the moving and unmoving of this world of mine is longing for Mother.

sṛṣṭiya pūrṇṇate illide kēḷū
satyam śivam sundaram

Here lies the fulfillment of Nature. Listen - 'satyam shivam sundaram'.

Nannōḍeya (Kannada)

nannōḍeya tiruka nānavana sēvaka
bhaktigē oliyuva sumanōpama sumukha

My Lord is a vagabond , and I am His servant. The One who is delighted by devotion, the One with a charming face...

himada baṇḍe masaṇabhūmi ella avana nivāsa
rāgabhōgagaḷigē avanu sadā udāsa
nondu benda hṛdayakkella karuṇāmṛta varuṣa

He lives in the mountains and cremation grounds. He has no taste for the materialistic world and its luxuries. He comes as a shower of compassion for the hearts that are in pain.

śīva śiva śiva hara hara hara śambhō śankara
śīva śiva śiva hara hara hara śambhō śankara

Shiva, Hara, Shambhu, Shankara!

jñānaghananu prēmamayanu mugddha saraḷa mahimanu
maruḷanante tōrutiha pracaṇḍa taraḷanu
ātmaratiyu mahāyatiyu bhaktajanage gatiyu

He is the embodiment of knowledge. He is love incarnate. He is simple yet great. He pretends to be foolish, but He is all knowing, and has great depth. He always revels in His own consciousness. He is the greatest monk and is the only hope for His devotees.

oṁ namaḥ śivāya oṁ namaḥ śivāya

Prostrations to Lord Shiva!

Orunāḷum piriyātta (Kannada version)

endendu ninagāgi hambalisi alede
huḍukāḍa deḍeyilla - amma
janmāntarakū jagadambe bēkentu
huḍukāḍa deḍeyilla - halajanma

gatigeṭṭa jīvitava nōḍu – enna
vijaya pratīkṣe baraḍāgide
taragele tharadali paravaśaḷāgi nā
dikkeṭṭu alediruvē – dāri, beḷakkāgi nī tōri bā

durmada ennali heḍe ettitō – ayyō
gati tappi naḍede durvidhiyindali
hagaliruḷēnnade hṛdayata ṭākadi
amṛtamaḷē surisū – amma, puḷaka rōmāncana tā

Neñcakaṁ ventiṭunnu (Malayalam)

neñcakaṁ ventiṭunnu – ammē
sañcitapāpa-tāpāl
vañcitanāyiṭunnu – innu
pañcēndriyaṅgaḷāl ñān

Mother, my heart is burning with the heat of accumulated sins. I am being betrayed by my five sense organs.

attal koṇḍende cittam – ēre
taptamāy nīriṭunnu
itramēl tāṅguvānāy – illa
kelppenikkantarangē

My heart is being seared with sorrow- I have no strength to withstand such pain.

en tāpaminnakattān – kṛpā-
sindhuvām nin hṛdantē
pontiṭēṇam-uṭanē – kṛpā-
vantiramālayonnu

To end my burning sorrow, a pure wave of kindness must arise from the ocean of compassion that You are.

Pādāravindakē (Kannada)

pādāravindakē namipēśāradē mātē

I bow down to Your lotus feet O Mother Sharada!

sangītalōlini sakala vidyādātē
viṣṇusahōdari varadē vāgīśvari

Lover of music, bestower of all knowledge, sister of Vishnu, Goddess of speech!

śvētāmbaradharē śāśvatē śubhadē
caturvēda caturē vīṇāpāṇi
nārada janani nādabrahmāṇi
nāmapārāyaṇāmṛta karuṇisammā...
nāmapārāyaṇāmṛta karuṇisammā...

You are adorned in white, O eternal auspicious One. Wise one, You know of the four Vedas, and play the veena. Mother of Narada (ancient immortal sage), Goddess of sound, kindly grant us the grace to incessantly chant Your names.

kāruṇyasindhuvē paripūrṇṇa bandhuvē
śraddhēbhaktiya nīḍi paripālisammā
mamakāra naśisi vairāgya mūḍisi
pariśuddha jñānava nīḍu nī namagē
pariśuddha jñānava nīḍu nī namagē

Ocean of compassion, complete, eternal friend. Please destroy our attachments, let detachment and renunciation dawn in us. This way, bestow on us pure knowledge.

sangītalōlini sakala vidyādātē
viṣṇusahōdari varadē vāgīśvari

Lover of music, bestower of all knowledge, sister of Vishnu, Goddess of speech!

Ponnammā en ammā (Tamil)

ammā undan tāy pāsam, dēsam ellām oḷi vīsum
rōjā malarin vāsam, undan varavai pēsum

Mother, the light of Your maternal affection is all-pervading. The fragrance of roses heralds Your arrival.

ponnammā en ammā sellammā nī ammā
pozhutellām unnōṭu nān irukkalāmā

O darling Mother, my Mother, may I spend my free time in Your presence?

kaivaḷaikaḷ kulunga kāl salangai siṇunga
suttri suttri azhakāy nī naṭanam āḍumpōdu
kaṇkuḷira un ezhilai nān rasikkalāmā?
mālaippozhutil marattadi nizhalil
manankavarum nal kataikaḷ nī uraikkum pōdu
kātinikka un mozhikaḷ nān kēṭkalāmā?

As Your bangles jangle and anklets clink while You dance enchantingly in circles, may I revel in Your refreshingly beautiful form? At night, in the shade of a tree, as You narrate captivating stories, may I listen to Your words, which are like music to the ear?

mazhalayai tūkki maḍiyinil amartti
makizhvuḍan un viralāl sōru ūṭṭumpōdu
nāvinikka un kaiyāl amudarundalāmā?
nakṣattira pandal kīzh nilavai nōkki nī
bhaktiyuḍan manamuruki pāṭal pāṭum pōdu
un bhakti mazhayil nān mey silirkkalāmā?

As You carry a child, place him in Your lap, and feed him, may I partake of the elixir from Your hand? Under the canopy of the starry sky, as You gaze at the moon and sing devotional songs that melt the heart, may I become ecstatically drenched in that rain of devotion?

Sāmbasadāśiva (Tamil)

sāmbasadāśiva sāmbasadāśiva
saccidānandanē sāmbaśivā

O ever auspicious Lord accompanied by Mother Shakti! You are the embodiment of existence-knowledge-bliss.

poyyāṁ ulakaṁ purindiṭavē
meyyāy unpadaṁ puṇarndiṭavē
nādan un mahimai pāṭukirēn
namaḥ śivāya ena kūrukirēn

To know the illusory nature of the world and to attain Your feet which itself is truth, I sing Your praises and chant 'Namah Shivaya.'

vēdattin nāyakanē dēvā
mādorubhāgan ānavanē
māl ayan kāṇā pēroḷiyē
ālayamāguṁ ānandamē
sāmba sadāśiva... sāmba sadāśiva...
sāmba sadāśiva... sāmba sadāśiva...

O Lord, You are the Leader of the Vedas, and share half of Yourself with Shakti. Your effulgent form was not seen even by Lord Vishnu and Lord Brahma. You are the bliss in which all beings merge.

Parinamamiyallatta (Kannada version)

pariṇāma villada paramēśvari - ena
paritāpa ninagē tiḷidillavē?
madanārī paramēśa patiyallave - ena
manadā iruḷannu kaḷeyamma nī

iruḷāgi kaḷēdu hagalallave – ena
iruḷantha hṛdayanina garivillave?
daḷavellā uduridā hūvādene?
daye tōralendu nī baralāreyā?

kirubaḷḷiga abhaya hem-maravallave? amma
kirumakkaḷ-abhilāṣe nīnallave?
nānēnu māḍali hēḷambikē
ninnalli ondāga bēkambikē

baraḍāda marubhuvil alediruvē nā – ammā
baralāradāgide nina sanihakke
nīḍamma enagendu dayadintali
nina pādadāśraya sarvveśvari

Śivke (Hindi)

śivke bāyē śōbhit śakti
tum deti hō bandan mukti
har jīvōm ke antaryāmi
tumre āgē mastak ṭekkum

Adorning Shiva on his left, You free us from bondage. O indweller of all beings, I bow down to You.

śivaśakti svarupiṇī, ānandarupiṇi, prēmasvarupiṇī māte

Mother, You are of the embodiment of Shiva-Shakti, of ananda (bliss) and of love.

nabh hai terā śīrsh bhavāni
dhartti pe tu per rakhī hai
sab jīvōm me cetan tuhi
bhavbādhā kō dur kare mā

With the sky as Your head, You keep Your feet on the earth. You are life in all beings. You remove of worldly sufferings.

jai māte, jai devi, jag māte, jagadambe...

Hail Mother, hail Goddess, hail Mother, O Mother of universe!

jananī terī sarjan kelī
bujhtti nā ye sṛṣṭi pahelī
tumhī jāne tatva anōkhā
nit nīrāgētup nirālā

O Mother, it is impossible to solve the riddle of Your creation. You alone know the wondrous essence of this ever changing creation.

bagtōm kō tu premamayī hai
dukhiyōm pe kāruṇya dikhātti
muniyōm mē tu gyān jagātti
danujōm kō niśśeṣ harātti

You are full of love towards Your devotees, and You shower Your compassion on the afflicted. You are the source of knowledge in the sages. You are the destroyer of evil.

Śri dēvi laḷitā (Tamil)

śri dēvi laḷitā paramēśvari
śricakraṁ vīttiṭum laḷitēśvari
ulakin annaiyē anpunāyaki
umai ambikē dēvi kanyākumari

You are Lalita Paramesvari who is Goddess of wealth and Supreme Goddess. You are Goddess Laliteshvari who resides in Sri Chakra. You are the Mother of Universe and the Queen of compassion. You are Goddess Uma Parasakti in the form a maiden.

kayalvizhi karuṇaimiku mīnākṣiyē
kāśipuraṁ jñānamaruḷ viśālākṣiyē

karimbuvillēntum kāmākṣiyē
arumbu malaraṭi śaraṇam tāyē

You are compassionate Goddess Meenakshi with fish shaped eyes. You are Goddess Visalakshi from the city of Kashi, bestowing knowledge. You are Goddess Kamakshi holding the sugarcane bow. O Mother! We take refuge at Your feet which are as soft as flower buds.

āyiram itazhmītē kamalāmbikē
ātmavidyaiyaruḷuṁ vimalāmbikē
anaittuyirai anpāl piṇaittavaḷē
anbu malaraṭi śaraṇam tāyē

You are the Goddess sitting on thousand petaled lotus. You are the Goddess giving the knowledge of Atman. You have connected all souls with love. We take refuge at Your feet that are like flowers of compassion

ūnamatai akattum umāśankariyē
vīṇai nādaṁ mīṭṭiṭuṁ maṇgaḷāmbikē
prāṇa śaktiyākum karppakāmbikē
praṇava rūpiṇi śaraṇaṁ tāyē

You are Goddess Uma Sankari who saves us from the cycle of birth and death. You are Goddess Mangalambika who plays the veena. You are Goddess Karpakambika who has become pranic energy. You are in the form of pranava - we take refuge in You.

śaraṇaṁ śaraṇam śaraṇam laḷitā paramēśvari
śaraṇaṁ śaraṇam śaraṇam gaurikṛpākari
śaraṇaṁ śaraṇam śaraṇam śrībhuvanēśvari
śaraṇaṁ śaraṇam śaraṇam rājarājēśvari

Mother Lalita, supreme Goddess, fair one, gracious one, supreme Empress of the universe, we take refuge in You!

Taḻarnnuraṅgukayō (Malayalam)

taḻarnnuraṅgukayō? iniyum
viṣādamūkatayō?
manujakōṭikaḷ viṣayagaraḷam
nukarnnuraṅgukayō! tammil
marannuraṅgukayō?

Why are you sleeping in exhaustion? Why are you so sad and depressed? Why are the millions of human beings imbibing the poison of materialism and sleeping? Why have they forgotten each other?

kālattin kaiviralttumbāl viracicca
chāyā citraṅgaḷō... manuṣyan
uyarttiyatalakaḷ! tāzhttiya talakaḷ
viraḷunna – viḷarunna mukhaṅgaḷ! eviṭeyum
maraviccu-maruvunna manuṣyan?

Are we just pictures drawn by the finger tips of time? Men with upright heads, men with downcast faces, pale and scared faces - everywhere men are living frigid lives.

niṅgalkku kaṇikāṇān niṅgaḷe kaṇikāṇān
innī jagattil manuṣyaruṇḍō?
uṇḍenkiloru tāmara-malarmoṭṭupōle
mizhiyaṭaccuraṅgunnatentē... hṛdayam
itaḷ-viṭarttīṭāttatentē?

Are there human beings in this world for you to see when you wake up? Are you there for them to see when they open their eyes? If so, why are you closing your eyes and sleeping like a lotus bud? Why does your heart not open up its petals and bloom?

Tañcam undan (Tamil)

tañcam undan pādamenṭru
śaraṇaṭaindēn dēviyē... nān śaraṇaṭaindēn dēviyē
neñcam undan kōyilenṭru
nī amarvāy dēviyē... adil nī amarvāy dēviyē

O Goddess, Your holy feet are my only refuge. I surrender to You. Make my heart Your temple. Please reside within my heart.

munnam seyda vinaikaḷ ellām
muṭṭimōdippārkkutē... enai muṭṭimōdippārkkutē
enna solvēn undan seviyil
ēzhaiyin kural kēṭkutā – inda ēzhaiyin kural kēṭkutā

The fruits of past actions are trying to torment me. What shall I tell You, O Mother? Please listen to the helpless musings of this poor one.

enda niramtān undan niramō
enakku colvāy dēviyē... nī enakku colvāy dēviyē
enda vaṭivam undan vaṭivō
eṭuttu colvāy dēviyē... nī eṭuttu colvāy dēviyē

O Goddess tell me which color is Your true color? O Devi, please show me which form Your true form is.

kaṇkaḷ ceyta payan anṭrō
kāḷi unnai kāṇpadu – annai kāḷi unnai kāṇpadu
paṇ amaittu pāṭum inda
bālanai nī kāttiṭu... inda bālanai nī kāttiṭu

Beholding Your form would be the true merit of having eyes. Please protect this child of Yours who is singing Your glories!

Tāṇḍavamāṭi (Tamil)

tāṇḍavamāṭi dayāpari varuvāy
dharaṇiyil piravippiṇi tīrkka
tāmarai malarmītē vīttiṭum mā dēvi
tāmarai idayattil naṭamāṭi vā kāḷi

Compassionate One, come dancing, to remove the cycle of birth and death! Mother Devi, sitting on lotus flower, Mother Kali! Come dancing to my lotus heart

vañcanaiyāl enkum adharmam perukutē
nañcāka koṭuñceyalē enkum vaḷarutē
kāḷiyāy vantu nī dharmam uṇarttavē
adharmmattai ozhittiṭa tāṇḍavamāṭi vā

Unrighteousness spreads everywhere due to deception. Cruelty grows everywhere like a poison. Come as Mother Kali to make us realize righteousness. Come dancing to remove unrighteousness!

jadi colli kavipāṭa kaḷiyāṭa manamāṭa
dēvi nīyō naṭanamāṭa
salankai kiṇukiṇunka virikūntalāka
kaṇṇāyirattāl āṭum tiruttāṇḍavam
dēviyāṭu... ādiparāśaktiyāṭu

My mind is in joy with rhythmically composed poems. O Mother Devi - You are dancing, with anklets tinkling and Your hair flowing freely. O thousand-eyed Goddess who dances so divinely! It is Mother Devi, primordial energy!

māyā svarūpiṇi māyaiyil vaśappeṭṭē
māyayai āṭṭivaikkum ādiparāśakti
manattirai vilakkiyē māyai kaṭattiṭavē
maṇṇulakil dharmam tazhaikka vanta tāy nī

You are the form of maya (illusion) and You at the same time You are under maya. You govern maya – O primordial One, You have come to Earth to unveil the mind and remove maya! In this way righteousness will flourish.

maṇṇāti uyirkaḷum makizhntē āṭiṭa
maṇṇilum viṇṇilum mankaḷam niraintiṭa
dēvādi dēvarum iśaimīṭṭi malar tūva
tiruḷḷattōṭu nī āṭum pukazhttāṇḍavam

For earthly beings to dance happily, for auspiciousness to fill the earth and heaven, for the showering of flowers to the sound of divine music by the gods- the dance You are dancing is a much-praised one!

Taye tava (Kannada version)

tāye ninna makkaḷali
kāruṇya tōrammā
tāpadi hṛdaya tapisutide
kāruṇya rūpāngane

mōda bandu divākara prabheyu
mareyāguvantē
mōhakkai siluki nāsōlladirali
kāruṇya rūpāngane

taruvu lateyū jalavu akhila
jīva jālagaḷū
nina sṛṣṭi entu nānintu arite
kāruṇya rūpāngane

Ulagamāga māri nirkkum (Tamil)

cētanā adhiṣṭhitam jagat sarvam
inda pārellām paramporuḷin palarūpangaḷ

The whole universe is supreme consciousness. All that we see in this universe are manifestations of this supreme.

ulagamāga māri nirkkum ulaga annaiyē
inda ulagam vēru nī vēru embatillaiyē
idanai ariyum nālvarayil amaidiyillaiyē
idai arinda pinnar arindiṭavē onṭrum illaiyē

O Mother who is both the universe and the universal Mother, You are not separate from this universe, You are the universe itself. There is no peace till one realizes this truth. Once one realizes this truth, there is nothing more to achieve in this world.

arindu seyyum pizhaikaḷum agalavē illaiyē
ariyāda pizhaikaḷum vilagavē illaiyē
unnai nānum arindiṭa vāyppum illaiyō
vidhiyai māttrum unnaruḷ enakkillaiyō

I have not been able to get rid of the errors committed knowingly, nor have the unknowingly committed errors ended. Is there no way I can realize You? Am I not worthy of Your grace to change my fate?

aṭankāda manadil nī oḷirvadē illaiyē
manadai aṭakkum vazhiyum teriyavē illaiyē
vāzhum nāṭlkaḷ ovvonṭrum undan maṭiyilē
un dayavanṭri vērēdum vazhiyum illaiyē

You don't shine forth in an uncontrolled mind- nor do I know how to control my mind. Every day of my life is on Your lap. There is no other way to obtain Your grace.

Ulakattin tāyenṭru (Tamil)

ulakattin tāyenṭru unaipōttriccolvārē
uttamarellōrum tāyē - atan
uṭkaruttariyēn un sēyē
uṭalukku tāyāka ulakattil palaruṇḍu
uyirukku tāyānatālē - enkaḷ
ulakattāy ānāyō nīyē

The great ones praise You as the universal Mother. The significance of this is not clear to this child. There are many biological mothers. Are You the universal Mother because You are the mother of life itself?

pullirkkum pūvirkkum bhuvitannil yāvirkkum
purikinḍra mozhiyonḍru tāyē - adai
purindanbai pozhipavaḷ nīyē
kallirkkum uḷḷēyum īrattai kaṇḍinku
kanivōṭu anaittiṭum tāyē - emmai
karaisērkkum tōṇiyum nīyē

There is one language understood by all beings in creation (love); knowing this, You shower love on all beings. O Mother, You lovingly embrace even the stone-hearted.You are the boat which takes us ashore from this ocean of samsara.

nimmatiyai tēṭi nirkkāmalē ōṭi
niraivinḍri māniṭam taḷarum - tan
ninaivizhandiravil kaṇ āyarum
tammirkkuḷ tāmākum tanitta annilaiyilē
tavarāmal nī vandaṇaippāy - amaidi
tarukinṭra muttam padippāy

Humanity is relentlessly running in a fruitless search for peace. Exhausted from this search, man enters the state of deep sleep.

In this state, where there is no duality, You unfailingly come and kiss us, bestowing peace upon us.

Unai maravā varamonḍru (Tamil)

unai maravā varamonḍru unniṭam kēṭṭēn – unai
enḍrum vaṇankiṭum nal manamonḍru kēṭṭēn

Please grant me a boon that I may never forget You. Grant me a heart that ever bows down to You.

sollonnā tūyarattil tūvaṇḍiṭum pōtum
cañcalankaḷ en manadai sūzhndiṭumbōtum
piravāda nilai kāṇa vazhiyinai kāṭṭi
piraviyadu kaṭaittēra padamalar taruvāy...

When my mind is tormented by endless sorrows, when desires engulf my mind, show me the way out of the cycle of birth and death by granting me refuge at Your lotus feet.

ulakirkku unaiyanṭri uyvadu uṇḍō
uyirukku unaiyanṭri uravadu uṇḍō
sērāda iṭam sērndu uzhanṭriṭum ennai
sērttiṭuvāy un pādakamalattil inḍru...
sērttiṭuvāy un pādakamalattil inḍru

Is there any refuge for the world other than You? Is there any near and dear one for this soul other than You? Even as I languish in the midst of unsuitable company, may You merge me unto Your divine feet.

manamōhana madhusūdhana rādhā ramaṇā
kaṇṇā kaṇṇā...

O Krishna of enchanting beauty, slayer of demon Madhu, beloved of Radha.

Uyara uyara (Tamil)

uyara uyara pōkum manam āzhntu pōkavē
sōrntu pōyviṭāmal atai nī kākkavē
vāzhkayil uttama tattuvam nī
makattuvam nirainta māmaṇi nī

The mind that is soaring upwards must also dive into the depths. While doing that, please protect me so that it will not lose vigor and become listless. O Master, You are the supreme truth in one's life. In You lies the pearl of excellence.

ganamāna ninaivukaḷ varumbōtellām
guruvē un vārttaikaḷ itamānatē
mārā vicāraṇai seytīṭavē
vairāgyaṁ nī tūṇḍa nalamākutē

Whenever I am in the throes of my own spiritual seeking, O Guru, Your words of comfort alone give me strength. You are instigating the determination in me so that the ceaseless enquiry will go on within.

anubhavamām peru vīthiyil naṭattum guruvē
pūvō vazhi muḷḷō viral piṭi pōtumē
ituvē nān nitaṁ seyyuṁ or prārtthanai
guruvē un aruḷ vākku balamānavai

In this expanded world of experiences, You are leading me on the path where there may be thorns and there may be flowers. No matter how the journey is, as long as You are holding onto at least one finger of mine, that is enough for me. This is my everlasting prayer to You. Please always give me strength with Your grace-filled words.

Uyirōṭuyirāy (Tamil)

uyirōṭuyirāy uṇarvōṭuṇarvāy
uravāṭiṭa vā kaṇṇā
siraiyil piranda maraiyin poruḷē
piravippayanē kaṇṇā

O Krishna! Come and be one with my being and consciousness. You, who were born in a prison, are the essence of the Vedas and the fulfillment of life.

pettravar anbum suttravar tuṇaiyum
uttravanum nī kaṇṇā
kattratu koṇḍu pattradu viṭṭu
pettradum unaiyē kaṇṇā...
pettradum unaiyē kaṇṇā

You are the embodiment of parental affection, of help from kith and kin. You are the intimate One. You are attained by dispassion that is obtained through knowledge.

akalāden manam tudittiṭum un padam
ānirai mēykkum kaṇṇā
ayarādoru kaṇam ninaittiṭum un mukham
ālilai tuyilum kaṇṇā...
ālilai tuyilum kaṇṇā

O Krishna, cowherd boy! My mind steadfastly worships Your feet. O Krishna who sleeps on the banyan leave! My mind tirelessly remembers Your face.

kaṇṇā... kaṇṇā... kaṇṇā... kaṇṇā...

O Kanna...

Vaṭavṛkṣmām (Malayalam)

vaṭavṛkṣmām ninnil paṭarān kotikkunna

oru ceruvalli ñān ammē...
onnu taḷiriṭṭu pūviṭum munpe nī
vēraruttīṭarutē... enne
vērōḍe nīkkarutē

I am a tiny creeper that yearns to climb the banyan tree that You are. Please do not uproot or tear me away before I sprout and flower.

etrayō nāḷayi ñān pūjiccu nin pādam
bhakti ennil ankuriccū...
taḷiriṭṭu pūviṭṭu kaniyāy nin padatāril
patiyānāy ennē anugrahikkū... ammē
patiyānāy ennē anugrahikkū

After worshipping You for so long, the bud of devotion has sprouted in my heart. O Mother, bless me so that I may sprout, flower and bear fruit, which can be offered at Your feet.

azhalinte veyilēttu vāṭumen taṇḍum
taḷirum nīyillāte pōyāl
viṭarātaṭarumen moṭṭukaḷ vyathayōḍe
kēzhum nīyillāte pōyāl... vāḍi
vīzhum nīyillāte pōyāl

If You don't come to me, my stem and leaves will wilt under the scorching heat of sorrow. My buds will wither away and fall even before blossoming.

picca naṭakkuvānāvātta kuññine
mātāvu kaiviṭṭu pōyāl...
oru tuḷḷi pālināy kēzhumā kuññinte
vazhiyentu? pizhayentendammē... piñju

kuññinte gatiyentendammē

O Mother, if You leave this toddling child, who is crying for a drop of milk, what will it do? What wrong did I do? What will the lot of this tiny babe?

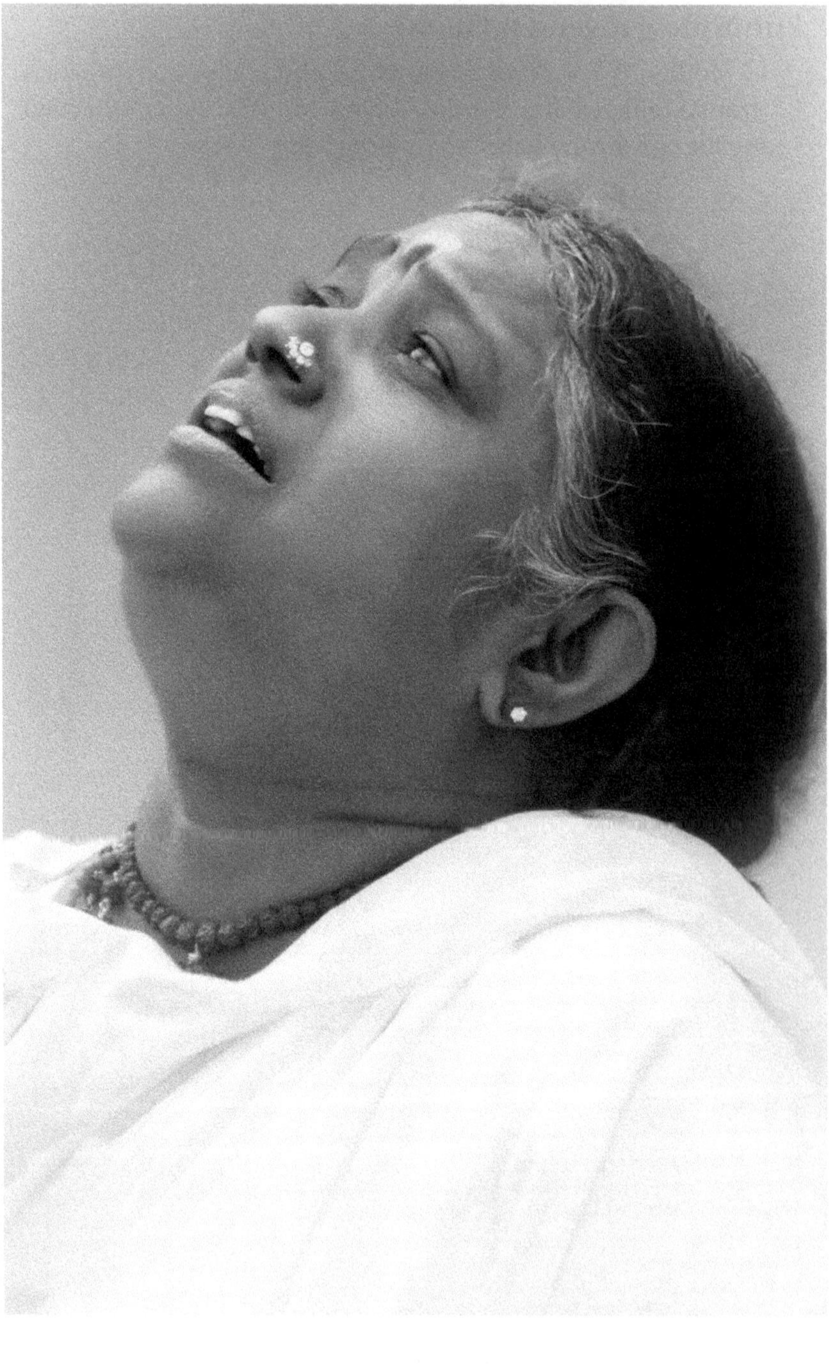